BEHOLD THE LAMB

ADVENT FROM THE GOSPEL OF JOHN

RAY PRITCHARD

Table of Contents

This Advent devotional guide comes from Keep Believing Ministries.

You can find us on the Internet at *www.KeepBelieving.com*.

Questions or Comments?
Email: *ray@keepbelieving.com*

Christmas Before Bethlehem

ADVENT FROM THE gospel of John?

Yes, but it's not the Christmas story we've heard before. John doesn't give us shepherds, mangers, or wise men. You won't find any mention of Caesar Augustus or a census that caused Joseph and Mary to make a difficult journey to Bethlehem.

No room in the Inn? That's in Luke, not John.

The star in the east? That's in Matthew, not John.

Good news of Great joy? Luke!

The nighttime journey to Egypt? Matthew!

The genealogies? Matthew and Luke!

Did John not know about those things? Yes, of course he did. But remember that he probably wrote his gospel in AD 90-95, a whole generation after the other gospels.

He didn't mention what Matthew and Luke had already covered.

The late Paul Harvey had a weekday radio program called "The Rest of the Story" that featured intriguing stories from history with unexpected endings. He closed each program the same way: "And now you know the rest of the story."

That's what John is doing for his readers.

He wants us to know "the rest of the story."

That's why we don't start in Bethlehem or Jerusalem, but in eternity past. John has a mind-blowing view of history. Before there was anything else, there was God!

That's where we have to start.

We're going to journey through John's gospel one day at a time. When we finally get to Christmas Day, we'll end with his stated purpose: *that you may believe that Jesus is the Christ, the Son of God.*

Get ready for an Advent journey unlike anything we've done before. Together, we're going to walk through John's Gospel, learning a little more about Jesus each day.

To help you go deeper, we'll post a daily video for each devotional. You can view those videos on Facebook, YouTube, X, LinkedIn, and the Keep Believing website.

Each devotional ends with a prayer and a link to a YouTube video of a Christmas song. I hope you'll take time to read the prayer aloud, then watch the video. Those two things will point your heart in the right direction.

Do you need some good news? Read on!

Let's get started on a journey that starts long before Bethlehem.

December 1

In the Beginning Was the Word

In the beginning was the Word, and the Word was
with God, and the Word was God.

— JOHN 1:1

CHRISTMAS STARTED LONG before Bethlehem.

Before the angels sang or Mary held Jesus in her arms, and long before the Wise Men journeyed to Jerusalem, there was the Word.

John's Christmas story doesn't mention a manger. His story starts in eternity.

"In the beginning was the Word." Before Caesar issued his decree, before Isaiah prophesied the Virgin Birth, before the shepherds saw the sky filled with angels, and before the Wise Men brought their gifts, before all of that, there was the Word.

Why does John call Jesus the Word? Think of it this way. Nothing is more invisible than a thought.

You don't know what I am thinking, nor can I tell what you are thinking. *But let a man speak, and his words reveal his thoughts.* Take the deepest thought and clothe it in words, and it will be visible to millions. Consider the plays of Shakespeare. They are the thoughts of Shakespeare made visible through his words.

Jesus reveals God to us. *He makes known what we would never discover on our own.*

The Babe of Bethlehem is more than a helpless infant. He is Almighty God in human flesh. The straw in the manger cradled the Creator of the universe.

Martin Luther said it this way:

> He whom the worlds could not enwrap
> Yonder lies in Mary's lap.

The baby wrapped in rags is also the King of Kings and the Lord of Lords. He's the Lion of the Tribe of Judah, the undefeated Son of God.

He's the leader of the armies of heaven.

This is Day 1 of our journey through John's Gospel. As we begin, take a moment to marvel that the infinite has become an infant, the Creator has joined his creation, the eternal has entered time.

God has moved into our neighborhood!

That baby is more than he seems. He is the Word from God and "the radiance of God's glory" (Hebrews 1:3). To quote the words of Charles Wesley (from "Hark! The Herald Angels Sing"):

> Veiled in flesh the Godhead see,
> Hail the incarnate Deity.

Either you believe that, or you don't. If you don't, then Christmas is just another day to you. But if you believe that, then you shouldn't have trouble believing anything else the Bible says.

When Jesus speaks, God speaks. May we have ears to hear what he is saying.

Lord Jesus, you are the Word made flesh. From everlasting to everlasting, you are God. As we begin this Advent journey, open our eyes to see your glory and worship you today. Amen.

Musical Bonus

Let's begin our musical journey with a beautiful rendition of the traditional Advent hymn *O Come, O Come, Emmanuel* by Maverick City. https://youtu.be/MtOi0IP0DCo

December 2

The Darkness Cannot Win

The light shines in the darkness, and the darkness
has not overcome it.
— JOHN 1:5

"Is DARKNESS A GOOD description of life without Christ?"

That's the question I asked my Wednesday night Bible class. One person spoke up and said, "Sure, because without him, you are lost in the darkness, and you don't know which way to turn."

Light has come!

That's the message of Christ in just three words. Isaiah 9:2 fills in the details:

The people walking in darkness have seen a *great light*; on those living in the land of *deep darkness* a light has dawned.

Deep darkness. What a perfect description of our world. It's in the headlines, in our communities, sometimes even in our own hearts. The world feels heavy, confusing, and divided. But John's opening words about Jesus remind us of something unshakable: *"The light shines in the darkness, and the darkness has not overcome it."*

Great light. That's Bethlehem, where blazing light from heaven filled the night skies. There was so much light that the shepherds were, to borrow an older phrase, "sore afraid." Scared and terrified is more like it.

That's what light does. When it shines, the darkness can't stay in the same room.

But that's not the end of the story.

Check out that present tense: "shines." Not "shone," as if Jesus came with the light but when he left, the light left with him. That same Jesus, mighty Savior, tiny baby in the manger, still shines today.

The darkness killed the light, or so it seemed for three days in Jerusalem. But early on Sunday morning, the Light of the World came shining out of the darkness of the grave.

Don't be surprised when the darkness attacks you.

That's the whole story of the Christian church. A young man goes to a college campus to share his faith. Cut down by an assassin in the middle of his talk, killed for his faith, and hated for his boldness. Did the darkness win? Perhaps in the moment it seemed that way. But millions heard the gospel at his memorial service.

Suddenly light blazes from tens of thousands of young Christians who said yes to Jesus Christ.

Take heart today. Darkness cannot win. Jesus Christ—the Light of the World—still shines, and someday soon, his glory will fill the whole earth.

Lord Jesus, shine your light into the dark corners of my heart. Help me reflect your love, courage, and truth wherever you send me. Thank you that no darkness—past, present, or future—can overcome you. Amen.

Musical Bonus

Andrew Peterson has given us a new melody to an older carol called *While Shepherds Watched Their Flocks*. Enjoy! https://youtu.be/f5NTGqYwL68

December 3
Children of God

But to all who did receive Him, to those who
believed in His name, He gave the right to
become children of God.
— JOHN 1:12

IT MIGHT BE THE most surprising prisoner letter we've ever received. It came from a man who read my book *An Anchor for the Soul* and wrote to say thank you.

The man had been on a long search for Jesus:

I have tried being a Baptist, and it didn't fit me. I tried being a Catholic and a Mormon and came up with the same feeling (it didn't fit).

No one has ever said that to me before. But if he couldn't find Jesus in organized religion, where would he find him?

I came to believe that all this time I've been looking for a person (Jesus Christ). I realized I was allowing religion to get in the way of my faith.

He's right about one thing. The answers we all seek are found in a person—Jesus Christ!

John 1:12 offers a simple outline of what it means to come to Christ for salvation:

"To all who received him." The way of salvation begins with a simple step: Receiving Christ as Lord and Savior. To receive Christ means to welcome him as an honored guest and to have him make your heart his home.

"To those who believed in his name." To believe means to trust or to rely upon. It's what you do when you lie on your bed at night. You put your full weight on the bed, knowing that it will hold you up. Trusting Jesus means resting all that you are upon all that he is.

The prisoner added this sentence: "All I need to do is believe in Jesus Christ." John would say Amen!

Believing in Jesus means trusting him so completely that if he can't take you to heaven, you aren't going to go there. But he can—and he will!

"He gave the right to become children of God." The word right means "honor" or "privilege." The moment you receive Christ into your life, God gives you the honor of becoming a member of His family.

How simple it is to come to Christ. We have made it difficult when God made it easy. The hardest part is reaching out with the hand of faith. If you want to know Jesus, all you have to do is reach out to him.

"But my faith is not strong," you say. God never asks if our faith is strong; he only requires that it rest on the Lord Jesus Christ. Even a trembling hand can receive a golden cup.

When you trust in Christ, he will welcome you into his family. Won't you come to Jesus?

My Lord, thank you for making the way of salvation so simple.
With all my heart, I am trusting you—now and forever! Amen.

Musical Bonus
Sometimes we need to hear a Christmas carol in a new way. Jeremy Camp offers us a contemporary arrangement of *O Little Town of Bethlehem.*
https://youtu.be/nZurXcfBZgA

Welcome to the Neighborhood

The Word became flesh and made
his dwelling among us.
— JOHN 1:14

I LOVE THE WAY Eugene Peterson paraphrases the first part of John 1:14, "The Word became flesh and blood, and moved into the neighborhood." *For 33 years, God moved into our neighborhood —or, as some would say, he lived in the 'hood.'* The NIV says he "made his dwelling among us." Some translations say that he "pitched his tent among us." That's actually very accurate because the Greek word for "made his dwelling" literally means to pitch a tent. It's the same word used for the Tabernacle in the Old Testament, which was a tent where the glory of God dwelt in the days before the Temple was built in Jerusalem. The Tabernacle was sometimes called the "Tent of Meeting" (Exodus 40:34) because it was the divinely appointed meeting place between God and man. In the same way—but in a much deeper sense—Jesus is the place where we meet God today.

In the Bible, three kinds of people lived in tents—shepherds, sojourners, and soldiers. They lived in tents because they never stayed in one place very long. Jesus lived in the "tent" of his humanity for 33 years. He, too, was a shepherd, a sojourner, and a soldier. He came to be the Good Shepherd, he came as a visitor from heaven, and he came as the Captain of our Salvation to defeat the devil once and for all.

Ponder that for a moment. The Almightiness of God moved in a human arm. The love of God now beats in a human heart. The wisdom of God now spoke from human lips. The mercy of God reached forth from human hands. God was always a God of love, but when Christ came to the earth, love was wrapped in human flesh.

He was neither invisible nor obscure.

See his little hands and feet; they are the hands and feet of God. Listen to him laugh; it is the laughter of God. Wipe the tears from his infant cheeks; you are wiping the tears of God.

Some things we understand and therefore believe. *Christmas is a miracle of another order.* We can think of a thousand other ways God could have done it. But God chose the unusual (a virgin birth) and the unlikely (a baby born in a stable) as his means of visiting our planet. As we ponder the meaning of it all, our theology leads us to mystery, and the mystery leads to wonderment. At Christmastime, like the Wise Men of old, we are invited to bring our gifts to Bethlehem and welcome God to our world.

Gracious Lord, you entered our world and brought light into our darkness. Welcome to our neighborhood! We hope you feel at home because we need you so much. Amen.

Musical Bonus
I found a newer song by Matthew West called *Because of Bethlehem.* The message reminds us that everything changed when Jesus moved into our neighborhood.
https://youtu.be/NOGV5jcu2Oo

What Does God Look Like?

No one has ever seen God, but the one and
only Son, who is himself God and is in closest
relationship with the Father, has made
him known.
— JOHN 1:18

WHAT DOES GOD LOOK like?

The Bible doesn't leave us to wonder about the answer to that question. *Nearly 2000 years ago, a baby was born in Bethlehem who forever answered that question.* If you want to know what God is like, look at Jesus. Hebrews 1:3 calls him the "shining forth of the glory of God."

Does God have a name? Yes. His name is Jesus. *In him, the abstract becomes concrete.* When I look at Jesus, all those theoretical ideas about God suddenly become reality.

- God now has hands.
- And feet.
- And eyes to see.
- Ears to hear.
- Lips to speak.
- God has a voice!
- He speaks a language I understand.

I see him touch a leper, and I know no one is too dirty for him.

I see him pause to speak to a beggar, and I know he's never too busy for me.

I see him feed the multitudes with loaves and fishes, and I know he can supply my needs.

I see him with the towel and the basin, and I know no job is too menial for him.

Finally, I see him hanging on the cross, suspended between heaven and earth, beaten, bruised, bloodied, mocked, scourged, spat upon, jeered, booed, hated, attacked, scorned, despised, rejected, and crucified. When I hear him cry out, "Father, forgive them for they know not what they do," I suddenly understand that Jesus died to turn his enemies into friends.

In Jesus, I discover a God who takes people seriously. He never treats people casually. He never brushes them off. He never says, "You're a loser." He's a God who cares enough to get involved in this ugly, twisted, unredeemed world.

What does God look like? Take a look at Jesus and you have your answer.

Lord Jesus, if you had not come, we would not know the Father. Open our eyes that we might see how much God loves us. Amen.

Musical Bonus

In this moving rendition of *Agnus Dei*, AOH Music revives the ancient prayer *"Lamb of God, who takes away the sin of the world."* With simple beauty and quiet reverence, it points us to Jesus—the Lamb who was slain and now reigns forever.

https://youtu.be/0EhM29rVRw0

Saved by the Blood

Behold, the Lamb of God,
who takes away the sin of the world!
— JOHN 1:29

EITHER THE LAMB DIES. Or the firstborn of the family dies.

The blood must be shed either way. You can read the story in Exodus 12.

Suppose you were an Israelite being asked to sacrifice your prized lamb and smear its blood on the door for all the neighbors to see. Would you do it? Or would you be embarrassed by such a thought?

Someone reading about the first Passover might say, "This story is absurd!" *But I assure you that it is entirely true.* Suppose an Israelite had refused to sacrifice a lamb. His firstborn would have died that night. Being a Jew could not save on that fateful night. It's not national origin that matters to God but faith in God's appointed way of salvation.

In the same way, it is not your religious affiliation that matters to God. It's not about being Catholic, Baptist, Lutheran, or Presbyterian. And it doesn't have anything to do with your education, your wealth, your status, your achievements, the money you've made, the awards you've won, and it certainly doesn't involve how many important people you know.

God wants to know one thing: "Do you have faith that the blood of Jesus can wash away all your sins?" Jesus is the Lamb of God who takes away the sin of the world (John 1:29). The blood of Jesus cleanses us from every sin (1 John 1:7). *What the Passover lamb represented in the Old Testament, Jesus fulfills in the New Testament.*

Where will you find such a lamb?

Look to the Cross! Gaze upon the bleeding form of the Son of God! Behold the Lamb of God, who takes away the sin of the world!

Jesus is the Lamb you need. He is God's Lamb for your sin.

Sleep on, Lamb of God. Snuggle tight to your mother's breast. The road from Bethlehem leads to the Cross.

Lord Jesus, you are the Lamb of God who takes away the sin of the world—my sin. You left heaven's glory to walk among us, to suffer, and to die so that we might live. Fill my heart with gratitude and faith that never fades. Amen.

Musical Bonus
When Twila Paris introduced *Lamb of God* in 1985, she gave the church a song that still moves hearts today. Its words remind us that the baby in the manger was born to be the Lamb who would die for us.
https://youtu.be/tbOOiaV1-AI

December 7
A Quiet Miracle

On the third day a wedding took place at Cana in
Galilee. Jesus' mother was there, and Jesus and his
disciples had also been invited to the wedding
— JOHN 2:1-2

TWO THINGS STAND OUT to me in the story of Jesus turning water into
wine. *First, Mary expects her son to do something about the wine running
out.* No doubt, for a long time, Mary had wanted to share the secret
about Jesus with others. She wanted them to know that he was no
ordinary child, that he was the "Son of the Most High" who will one
day establish a kingdom that never ends. But that grand achievement
seemed very remote on that day in the little village of Cana when the
wine ran out before the wedding was over.

Second, we see in this miracle the hidden power of our Lord. As far
as we know, he never touched the water jars or said, "Let the water be
turned to wine." He didn't pray an audible prayer. He didn't announce
his intentions. He simply willed the miracle, and it came to pass.

First there was water.

Then there was wine.

It was a quiet miracle, completely unexpected.

But there is more.

There was plenty of wine for everyone. He provided "good wine."

Jesus not only meets the need, he goes above and beyond. When
Jesus comes to the party, no one goes home thirsty.

Here is good encouragement for the fearful. The same Lord who
willed the water to become wine can help you in your time of need. He
will never leave you nor forsake you.

If you need a miracle today, take heart. He can do what others call
impossible. He is the "above and beyond" Savior.

Mary will live to see her wish come true as multitudes believe in Jesus. But for now, this first miracle brings joy to a wedding feast. Those who understand believe in him.

A "quiet miracle" saved the day at Cana. It is a harbinger of much more to come.

Lord Jesus, open our eyes to see you at work all around us. Thank you for joy that can never be taken away. Amen.

Musical Bonus

First recorded by Selah in 2016, *Good Christian Men, Rejoice (Born to Reign)* breathes new life into one of the oldest carols in the Christian tradition.

https://youtu.be/8bdEPpaMGww

December 8
The Snake in the Desert

Just as Moses lifted up the snake in the desert, so
the Son of Man must be lifted up.
— JOHN 3:14

MOST OF US KNOW John 3:16.

Let's go back two verses and see what leads to that most famous of all the biblical promises. "Just as Moses lifted up the snake in the desert, so the Son of Man must be lifted up" (John 3:14). The first part of that verse refers to a strange moment in Israel's history recorded in Numbers 21. There we learn that during the wilderness wanderings, the people began to murmur against God and Moses by saying, "Why have you brought us up out of Egypt to die in the wilderness?" (v. 5).

After 40 years in the wilderness, the Jews were tired of the heat, the sand, and the long marches from one place to another. Even the manna seemed disgusting to them.

They were ready to go back to Egypt. Can you believe that?

Back to Pharaoh. Back to slavery. Back to oppression.

But that's what happens when you forget God and start taking your blessings for granted.

God heard their complaint and sent fiery snakes among the people. Many were bitten and many died. As panic swept across the tribes, the people came to Moses and said, "We were stupid to complain after all that God has done for us. Please pray to the Lord that he would remove these poisonous snakes."

When Moses prayed to the Lord, he was instructed to make a bronze snake and put it on a tall pole where the Israelites could see it: "Make a snake and put it up on a pole; anyone who is bitten can look at it and live" (v. 8). And that's what happened. Anyone who looked, lived. Those who didn't, died.

What is the significance of the serpent? Recall that sin entered the human race through the serpent that deceived Eve (Genesis 3:1-6). Ordinarily, lifting a snake on a pole would be repulsive to the Jews. In this case, it meant lifting the symbol of the very thing that was killing them.

John used this vivid image to teach us what the death of Christ really means. God took the hated symbol of Roman oppression (the cross) and turned it into the means of our salvation.

God has no other plan of salvation. Though some are offended by the bloody cross of Christ, those who look to Jesus are saved forever.

Look and live! That's the gospel invitation.

O God, you could not have made it any simpler. Forgive us for complicating the message of salvation. May multitudes look to Jesus and be saved today. Amen.

Musical Bonus
Avalon's *We Are the Reason* draws us into the heart of the Gospel message: God so loved the world that He gave His Son.
https://youtu.be/cMhajmOBr0c

December 9
The Hardest Question

Do You Want to Get Well?
— JOHN 5:16

CHANGE IS SCARY.

Sometimes it's easier to stay the way you are.

Jesus had come to Jerusalem during one of the yearly feasts. Thousands of pilgrims came from throughout Israel. While he was there, he paid a visit to a place called Bethesda, "the house of mercy." It was a pool near the Sheep Gate in the northeastern section of the city. Five colonnades (or porches) were built by the pool. As one writer put it, it was the Jewish Lourdes of that day. The Jews believed that an angel would periodically come and stir the waters. The first person to enter the water after it had been stirred would be healed of his diseases.

So hundreds of sick people gathered around the pool, waiting and hoping for the water to be stirred. On the day that Jesus passed by, he met a man who had been an invalid for 38 years. When he found out how long the man had been paralyzed, he asked only one question: "Do you want to be well?"

On the surface, it seems to be a bizarre question. Why else would the man be there? *Of course, he wanted to be well.* Was Jesus insulting his intelligence? No, not at all. He was asking a very serious question because it was entirely possible the man did not want to get well.

The man answers something like this: "Do I want to be healed? That's a crazy question. You must be new here. You don't understand the problem. Every time the water is stirred, somebody else beats me to it. No one will ever help me. They just push me out of the way. Have you ever heard a sadder story? Ain't it a shame!"

Jesus is probing at the level of the will. He's forcing the man to realize that as long as he blames others for his problems, he'll never get better. Change is scary because you get comfortable with the status quo even when you know your life is messed up. It takes courage to ask Jesus to change you. Sometimes it's easier to stay the way you are.

Jesus is saying, "Do you really want to be changed?" *If the answer is yes, then miracles can happen.* If the answer is no, then even Jesus can't help you.

Thank you, Lord, for being the Divine Disturber of the Peace.
For too long we have made excuses for the way we are. We truly
do want to get well. Heal us, O Lord. Amen.

Musical Bonus
I found a traditional carol with an Irish flair.
Check out this rollicking version of *God Rest Ye Merry, Gentlemen* by the Gettys.
https://youtu.be/4UItMqYFjsk

December 10

Jesus, The Great Divider of Men

We have never heard anyone speak like this!
— John 7:46

Here's the scene.

Jesus has come to Jerusalem to take part in the annual Feast of Booths. *As he speaks in the temple courts, thousands of pilgrims listen to his words.* They are excited and perplexed by his teaching. Some of them have heard about this upstart rabbi from Galilee. Word spreads quickly that the Pharisees want to kill him. But why were the rulers letting him teach openly? Why not just put him to death? Could it be that the leaders secretly think that he is the Messiah? Or maybe they're not sure themselves.

John tells us that many who heard him believed in him. When word reached the Pharisees, they sent the temple guards to arrest him. At that precise moment, Jesus made his famous declaration, "If anyone is thirsty, let him come to me and drink," and "streams of living water will flow from within him." There were three reactions to these statements: Some thought he was the prophet Elijah. Others correctly surmised that he was the Messiah. But a third group had questions about his ancestry. *How could he be the Christ since the Messiah must come from Bethlehem and not from Galilee?* Then John adds this sentence: "Thus the people were divided because of Jesus" (John 7:43).

The temple guards returned empty-handed. When asked why, they answered, "We have never heard anyone talk like this." Here is unimpeachable testimony from those who were sent to arrest him. *Yet his words arrested them!* They weren't believers, but they weren't sure either. Who is this man? Why does he speak this way?

In this episode, we see the true power of the Son of God. His enemies have no answer for him. He baffles his critics, even while they plot to take his life.

Two thousand years have passed, and Jesus still divides people today. Some believe, others don't. At Christmastime, we are invited to come and worship the newborn King. Will you bow before the Babe of Bethlehem this year?

Lord Jesus, never has any man spoken as you did. You stand alone among all those who have walked on the earth. Praise to you, O Lord, for you have confounded the wisdom of man and brought it to nothing. Amen.

Musical Bonus
First sung by believers more than 1,500 years ago, *Let All Mortal Flesh Keep Silence* calls us to stand in holy awe before the mystery of the Incarnation. Let's listen to this modern version of an ancient carol by Reawaken Hymns.
https://youtu.be/lNVCDNKbVFw

December 11
Neither Do I Condemn You

Did no one condemn you?
— JOHN 8:10

THIS IS THE STORY of the woman caught in adultery. Dragged before Jesus by the oh-so-righteous religious leaders, she waits to hear the inevitable verdict.

Stone her!

That's what the law demands.

But in the end, she walks away free and forgiven because when Jesus is finished with the religious mafia, there was no one left to accuse her of anything. At one point Jesus stooped to write something in the dust. *No one knows what he wrote.* Some have speculated that he wrote the names of the girlfriends of the accusers. It's more likely that he wrote Bible references to verses warning about bearing false witness.

One thing is clear. The men didn't care about the woman one way or another. *They were using her to trap Jesus.* She was the "bait," not the intended victim. But Jesus turned the tables on them by exposing their hypocrisy.

"Let the one without sin cast the first stone."

Motives matter.

In essence, Jesus is saying, "Before you pick up that stone, take a good look in the mirror. Make sure you are morally qualified to put this woman to death. Make sure there is no malice, no deceit, no trickery, no dishonesty, and make sure you are not guilty of the same crime yourself." He is reminding them that if they testify maliciously or deceitfully, they are signing their own death warrant.

The order of Christ's words in John 8:11 is critical. He didn't say, "Sin no more, and then I won't condemn you." That's what religious people like to say: "Clean up your act and then we will accept you." Jesus says, "I will forgive you and give you the power to clean up your act."

Religion says, "Change or I will condemn you." *It uses fear and intimidation to make people measure up.* Grace says, "I have forgiven you. Now let me also change your life."

We don't change in order to be accepted; we change because we have already been accepted. *Nothing motivates a new life like grace received into the heart.* Grace does what rules can never do.

The Savior speaks the same words today that he spoke so long ago: "Neither do I condemn you. Go and sin no more."

Lord Jesus, they called you the "Friend of Sinners," and so you are. You are the friend, and we are the sinners. Thank you for mercy that flows like a river from your bloody cross. Glory to your name forever. Amen.

Musical Bonus
This is perhaps the most stunning Christmas song I've ever heard. It carries the unlikely title of *O Come All You Unfaithful.* Listen and let the Good News give you hope.
https://youtu.be/C-QHbpYjuIg

December 12
Light of the World

Again Jesus spoke to them, saying, 'I am the light
of the world. Whoever follows me will not walk in
darkness, but will have the light of life.'
— JOHN 8:12

IN 1646, THE DUTCH artist Rembrandt created a painting called "The Adoration of the Shepherds." It depicts his vision of what it was like for the shepherds to see the baby Jesus. *The painting is dark because it is a night scene inside a barn.* The dark tones force the viewer to study the images carefully. In the center is the Babe in the feeding trough. Mary is by his side, Joseph not far away. The shepherds are gathered around, intently studying the baby whose birth was announced by the angelic choir. If you look into the gloom, you can see outlines of the sheep. The shepherds couldn't leave their sheep outside, so they brought them into the barn with them. To the right, a rickety ladder leans on a crossbeam. Next to the ladder is a rooster.

Soon it hits you that the ladder and crossbeam make the dim outline of a cross. The rooster symbolizes betrayal in the distant future. *Even in this joyous moment, the cross looms over the baby Jesus.* But the most significant feature is the light. Unlike other Renaissance artists, Rembrandt didn't paint Jesus as an angel with a halo. He is a very normal, very human baby. All is dark in the painting except for the baby in the manger. The light isn't shining on the baby; it's shining out from him. This was Rembrandt's way of saying that hope shines from the manger—lighting up a darkened world. These familiar words say it well:

Silent night, holy night,
Son of God, love's pure light

Radiant beams from Thy holy face,
With the dawn of redeeming grace,
Jesus, Lord, at Thy birth,
Jesus, Lord, at Thy birth.

Is there hope in the world? Yes! Hope invaded the world 2000 years ago at Bethlehem. If we want that hope to invade our lives, we must do what the shepherds did so long ago. We must come to Bethlehem and bow before the newborn King. Hope is available but only to those who will humble themselves and bow in faith before the Lord Jesus Christ.
Will you bow before him and crown him as your King?

Lord Jesus, there will always be room in my heart for you! Amen.

Musical Bonus
Sometimes the simplest voices carry the deepest truth. In this tender performance, American Idol winner Iam Tongi joins the Rexburg Children's Choir to sing *Silent Night*.
https://youtu.be/coHkcVafU-o

December 13
Now I See

One thing I do know, that though
I was blind, now I see.
— JOHN 9:25

HOW CAN YOU PROVE your faith is real?

The man born blind faced that problem when the Pharisees questioned him. They doubted everything about his story, including the fact that he had been born blind. But mostly they wanted to discredit Jesus, who had given him sight.

When facing a skeptical world, we can't always prove what we know to be true because spiritual truth is a matter of perception, not proof. How do you "prove" the beauty of a sunset? You can't. Either you see it, or you don't. That's like asking a young man to "prove" he is truly in love. Some things in life must be experienced to be understood.

This blind man doesn't know who Jesus is. He only knows what Jesus did for him: "I was blind, but now I see!" That was enough for him, even if it didn't convince the Pharisees. J. C. Ryle explains the importance of this sort of personal testimony:

"There is no kind of evidence so satisfactory as this to the heart of a real Christian. His knowledge may be small. His faith may be feeble. His doctrinal views may be at present confused and indistinct. But if Christ has really wrought a work of grace in his heart by His Spirit, he feels within him something that you cannot overthrow" (*Expository Thoughts*, vol. 4).

It reminds me of John Newton's testimony. After years spent as a slave trader, with no thought given to the Lord, he had a dramatic conversion when his ship began to founder during a terrible storm.

He left the slave trade and later entered the ministry. He wrote nearly 300 hymns, most of which have been long forgotten. But he wrote one hymn that is still sung around the world:

> Amazing Grace, How sweet the sound
> That saved a wretch like me
> I once was lost, but now am found
> Was blind but now I see.

That's the power of God.
That's true conversion.
That's the difference Jesus makes.

Do you know Jesus? Have you ever been converted? If so, do what this blind man did and let the world know. You don't have to "prove" anything.

Just tell what Jesus has done for you.

Lord Jesus, may I always be ready with an answer when someone asks, "What has Jesus done for you?" Amen.

Musical Bonus
While researching this project, I came across a song that, strictly speaking, is not a Christmas song. But it perfectly fits our theme. Let's listen to Cece Winans' rousing version of *That's My King*.
https://youtu.be/cM5qFXQ0p1o

The Shepherd We Need

I am the good shepherd. The good shepherd lays
down His life for the sheep.
— JOHN 10:11

HEROD WOULD NOT BE impressed.

After all, Herod was a king.

Kings and shepherds didn't mix.

Kings were, well, they were *Kings!* No self-respecting king would ever call himself a shepherd. That was reserved for people who couldn't find any other work.

When Joseph's family moved to Egypt, they were given the land of Goshen because the Egyptians despised shepherds (Genesis 46:33-34).

We forget that shepherds were near the bottom of ancient Israel's social order. They were often poor, uneducated, and quite young. Few people would pick "shepherd" on their Career Preference Form.

But Abraham was a shepherd, and so was Jacob. Moses shepherded his father-in-law's flock in the wilderness. David tended his father's flock on the fields near Bethlehem.

In the first century, many shepherds turned out to be hirelings who worked for the money but ran away at the first sign of danger, leaving the flock unprotected.

But a good shepherd was different. He stayed when wolves prowled and storms rolled in. His life was bound up with his sheep.

Jesus even told a story about a shepherd who had a hundred sheep, but when one of them went missing, he left the ninety-nine in the pasture and risked everything to find the one that was missing (Luke

15:3-7). He even put the sheep on his shoulders and joyfully carried it home.

We are like that one lost sheep. Centuries before Christ, Isaiah summed up the human condition this way: "All we like sheep have gone astray" (Isaiah 53:6).

We desperately need a Good Shepherd to come for us, to find us, and to lead us to safety.

Our Good Shepherd proved his love at the price of his own blood. He spent his first night on earth in a manger, which is a nice word for a feeding trough, the kind that shepherds used to feed cattle.

The Good Shepherd knows his sheep; he calls them by name, leads them to shelter, and protects them from the wolves that would destroy them.

If that doesn't convince you, remember this. Jesus didn't run from the cross. He could have called the angels of heaven to deliver him, and all the forces of Rome could not have captured him.

He went straight to the cross and gave himself for you and me.

That's our Good Shepherd.

Do you feel forgotten?

Keep going, keep believing, keep serving, keep giving. The Good Shepherd has his eyes on you.

Lord Jesus, thank you for being my Good Shepherd. Keep me close to your side today. When I wander, bring me home again. Amen.

Musical Bonus
Let's listen as Greater Vision gives us a new Christmas song called *Grace Has a Face*.
https://youtu.be/YlFALRULf9k

December 15
The Lord of Life

I Am the Resurrection and the Life.
— JOHN 11:25

NOTICE HOW PERSONAL this is.

Jesus doesn't say, "I *bring* resurrection and life," but rather, "I *am* the resurrection and the life." In the presence of Jesus, death is no longer death. It is something else entirely. As Paul says later in the New Testament, death has now lost its sting, and the grave its victory.

How can that be? The answer seems to be that Jesus himself has transformed death. I remind you that our Lord often used the word "sleep" to describe death. When he saw Jairus' daughter, he said, "The child is not dead but sleeping" (Mark 5:39). When he told the disciples that Lazarus was asleep (John 11:11), they were relieved because then they knew he would eventually wake up.

Sleep is natural and normal, which is why no one calls the paramedics when you lie down to take a nap. The whole point of sleeping is to wake up later. *Death for the believer is like lying down for a good, long nap.* The body may sleep for a long time—for many years, in fact—but in the end, it will wake up. When Jesus raised Lazarus, it was just a specimen, a sample of what he will do for his people when he returns to the earth.

A friend who watched a loved one die said it succinctly in just two words: "Death stinks." Yes, it does, which is why the Bible says death is the last enemy that shall be destroyed (1 Corinthians 15:26).

You can be released from the fear of death. But there's a question you must answer. It's the question found at the end of verse 26. We generally overlook the question, but it's the key to what Jesus said. When I've asked people to quote the passage, they always stop before the question. But if you skip the question, then you miss the whole point.

Here's the question. "Do you believe this?" Truth must always become personal. So I ask you, "Do you believe that Jesus is the resurrection and the life?"

If you know Jesus, you need not fear death.

It's a grand thing to be a Christian when you die.

Lord Jesus, what would we do without you? Where could we go but to the Lord? You alone have the words of eternal life. Thank you for giving us hope that death cannot destroy. Amen.

Musical Bonus
Phil Wickham brings a fresh burst of celebration to *Joy to the World (Joyful, Joyful)*. This rendition turns a familiar carol into overflowing Christmas joy.
https://youtu.be/DtrnuG5wZ-Y

The Magnetic Christ

> Now among those who went up to worship at the feast were some Greeks. So these came to Philip, who was from Bethsaida in Galilee, and asked him, 'Sir, we wish to see Jesus.'
> — JOHN 12:20-21

YOU NEVER KNOW WHO'S going to show up for a party.

In this case, some Greeks showed up in Jerusalem for the Passover Feast. In our day, that would mean "men from Greece," and it could mean that in this case. But in New Testament times, the term "Greeks" covered all the non-Jews, i.e., the Gentiles. These aren't Greek Jews who came for the big event. They are Gentiles from who knows where who have come to Jerusalem to join in the worship. That probably puts them in the category of Gentiles who became Jewish converts, or perhaps they were "God-fearers" (like Cornelius in Acts 10) who offered prayers to God and showed kindness to the poor.

Why did they want to see Jesus?

No doubt they were fully aware of the ruckus Jesus created when he cleansed the temple. We know the whole city was talking about him. If Twitter had existed back then, #WhoisJesus would have been a trending hashtag. Who was this man who could walk on water, heal the sick, and raise the dead?

Here is part of the answer: "I, when I am lifted up from the earth, will draw all people to myself" (John 12:32).

He is thinking of his coming death on the cross. Certainly, these unnamed Greeks were included in the "all people." Even before the cross, we see the magnetic power of Christ.

This should give us hope for our friends and loved ones. We can't know what other people are thinking. If we could see the hearts of our loved ones, we would discover that the Holy Spirit is at work, even though they seem far from Jesus today.

Don't despair.

Don't stop praying.

One final note. As a young man, I listened to Dr. Lee Roberson preach the gospel at Highland Park Baptist Church in Chattanooga, Tennessee. On the pulpit, just above where he placed his Bible and notes, there was a little plaque that said, "Sir, We would see Jesus." He put it there to remind himself (and anyone else who might preach there) of the preacher's sacred obligation to magnify Christ in all things.

There are hungry hearts everywhere. You never know when someone will show up looking for Jesus. Make sure you know how to help them find him.

Lord Jesus, thank you for opening the door of heaven to anyone who believes in you. Give me faith to keep praying for my friends who do not yet know you. Amen.

Musical Bonus
Here's a newer Christmas song called *How Many Kings* by downhere. Enjoy!
https://youtu.be/zF952rzG3Yk

December 17
Stinky Feet

Do you understand what I have done for you?
— JOHN 13:12

DIRTY FEET STINK.

That's a human fact, not a cultural observation. After a long, hard day, your feet have absorbed a pounding. If you wear sandals, they have been exposed to dirt everywhere. If your feet are in socks, they are probably sweaty. And then you have all the usual foot problems--ingrown nails, corns, calluses, cracked heels, and for some people, fungus of various kinds.

In those days, you normally washed your own feet after the host offered you a basin of water. You knelt, removed your sandals, washed your feet, and then dried them with a towel. If a man had servants, they might be delegated to do the job. This was the mark of high achievement in society: that servants washed the feet of your guests. *But under no circumstances would the host wash his guests' feet.* The master would never stoop so low as to wash the feet of those beneath him.

Slaves washed feet.

Masters never did.

That's why Peter is shocked when Jesus stoops down and begins to wash the feet of his disciples. Everything was upside down! They should be washing his feet; he shouldn't be washing *theirs*.

Jesus came to a world of dirty feet.

Our journey through life is much dirtier than we think. You never know what you might step in that will leave you defiled and unclean. We don't like to think about that, but it is true. No matter how hard we may try to stay clean, we are all dirtier than we think, and we end each day dirtier than when we started.

That's why Jesus told Peter that, although he was already clean, he still needed his feet washed. "A person who has had a bath needs only to wash his feet" (v. 10). Two different words are used here--one meaning a complete bath and the other meaning to wash something. *Coming to Christ is like taking a bath.* Our sins are washed away.

But we still need daily cleansing.

When we come to Christ, the guilt of our sin is removed forever. Because we live in a dirty world, we need cleansing every day.

Regeneration cannot be repeated.

Cleansing must be repeated.

We are great sinners who need a great Savior. We have one in Jesus Christ, who stooped so low that he was not ashamed to wash our dirty feet.

Lord Jesus, thank you for your blood that washes away my sin. I ask you to wash my dirty feet so I might walk closely with you today. Amen.

Musical Bonus
Keith and Kristen Getty have led a revival in contemporary worship music. Let's listen to their rendition of *Joy Has Dawned / Angels We Have Heard on High.*
https://youtu.be/lbbSJC9H2V4

December 18
The Only Way to Heaven

I am the way.
— JOHN 14:6

WE LIVE IN A "postmodern" age.

If that term is new to you, it simply means that we live in an age in which our culture has largely abandoned the notion of truth. The old consensus about right and wrong has almost entirely disappeared, replaced by appeals to pluralism, diversity, and moral relativism.

Against the spiritual confusion of our day, consider these "exclusive" claims regarding Jesus Christ:

A. He is the only Son of God–John 3:16.
B. He is the only name by which we can be saved–Acts 4:12.
C. He is the only way to the Father–John 14:6.
D. He is the only mediator between God and man–1 Timothy 2:5.
E. He is the only sacrifice for sin–Hebrews 10:12.

These statements demand a response. We have no right to water them down. You may choose to reject them or to call them "narrow-minded" or to pass them off as not applying to us today, but the fact remains that the Jesus of the Bible is an utterly exclusive Savior. He stands alone, and no one can compare with him.

When it comes to Jesus, too many people have a "hand grenade" faith. They think that "close" is good enough. Wrong!

Almost everyone believes in Jesus a little bit. That is, they believe in Jesus plus something else. But when you scratch under the surface, they don't believe in Jesus alone as their only hope of salvation. But to believe in him 95% is to be 100% lost.

Because Jesus is the only way to God, let me share with you five words that will take you all the way to heaven. If you take these five words to heart, and make them part of your life, if you will say them and believe them and rest upon them, these five words will take you to heaven when you die:

Jesus only and only Jesus!

Lord Jesus, you are the only Savior because you alone can save us.
We need no one else, and indeed, we have no one else besides you.
Thank you for making a way for sinners to be saved. Amen.

Musical bonus
Casting Crowns gives us a new version of the spiritual *Sweet Little Jesus Boy.*
https://youtu.be/wg7XprwTO5w

My Peace I Give You

Peace I leave with you; my peace I give you. I do not give to you as the world gives. Do not let your hearts be troubled and do not be afraid.
— John 14:27

Peace is a fantastic concept, and "my peace" is even better.

Peace is man's highest hope and his fondest dream. Most days it seems so hard to achieve. When Christ was born, the angel proclaimed, "Peace on earth, goodwill to men," but after 2,000 years, it still seems in short supply.

The Hebrew word for peace is *shalom*. If you visit Israel, people on the street will greet you with "Shalom!" "Peace to you, my friend." It is a mistake to think of *shalom* as simply being the absence of conflict. It is a much richer idea than that. Biblical *shalom* involves things like prosperity, happiness, contentment, and most of all, blessing from the Lord.

Peace is not the absence of trouble, but the presence of God.

It occurs to me that the only truly happy people I have ever known are those who have prayed, "Thy will be done." They have the "great peace" of Psalm 119:165. They have discovered that the way to peace is to yield everything to the Lord. Until you do that, there will be continual inner unrest.

Christians ought to be the calmest people on earth because we know the Lord, and he holds the future in his hands. The Lord is seated on his throne. He's not pacing the floor, wondering what will happen next.

When chaos breaks out on earth, perfect peace reigns in heaven.

In a practical sense, what should this mean for us? *First, we need to return to the Lord.* That's where we must begin. It does no good to point our fingers at people who disappoint us. Take a good look in the mirror. What do you see? It's time for all of us to get serious about our Christian faith.

Second, we need to release our anxiety. Why live in fear when Jesus has promised never to leave us? Let's live as men and women of hope. A businessman was on a long flight home when the airplane hit turbulence. Thunder cracked, and high winds blew the plane up and down, like a cork bobbing on the water. Lightning flashed across the skies. When the man looked around, he saw his fellow passengers were terrified. But then he noticed a young girl who seemed unconcerned. She tucked her feet under her seat and calmly read a book. When the plane finally landed, the businessman asked her why she wasn't frightened. "My father is the pilot," she replied, "and he's taking me home."

That's the faith we need in these uncertain days. Our Father is the pilot, and he will make sure we get home safely.

Lord, you are the giver of perfect peace. Help me to cast all my cares upon you. May your calm spirit rule my thoughts today. Amen.

Musical Bonus
In a smooth, soulful pop style, Christian Paul reimagines *The First Noel* with heartfelt reverence and quiet joy.
https://youtu.be/FjC8njCFWfM

December 20
Stay Close to Jesus!

I am the vine: you are the branches. If you remain
in me and I in you, you will bear much fruit;
apart from me you can do nothing.
— JOHN 15:15

"PASTOR RAY, WHAT'S THE secret of the Christian life?"

I've heard that question so many times in so many places, asked by so many people in so many ways.

We all want to know how to live the Christian life effectively—and even victoriously.

Is there a secret?

Perhaps I can state my answer this way. I've been a Christian for 56 years, since the day I trusted Jesus as my Savior at 16. Since then, I've heard many "secrets" that people promise will help you grow as a Christian. All of them have some value.

If there is a "secret" we need to know, it's right here in our verse for today. If Jesus is the vine and we are the branches, our one job—our only job—is to remain in him. Older versions use the word "abide," but the meaning is the same.

Just as I was typing these words, I took a break and started pruning back the rose bushes in our front yard. All summer we had beautiful flowers, but they are long gone. With winter upon us, the time has come to cut back the bushes so that they will grow back with more roses next summer.

So it is with you and me. From time to time, the Lord must do some "pruning" of our souls so that we may produce the beautiful fruit of Christlike character. It isn't easy, and it certainly isn't fun or painless, but pruning is necessary if we are to become all God wants us to be.

In all of this, we have only one job. One task. One assignment.

Stay close to Jesus.

Remain in him.

Everything else is details.

Apart from him, we can do nothing.

But all things are possible through Christ.

Advent offers us a challenge: to slow down, recalibrate our spiritual life, and return our focus to the Lord.

Stay close to Jesus! That's the real secret of the Christian life.

Heavenly Father, help us to remain connected to Jesus, abiding in his love and his Word. Prune away anything in our lives that keeps us from bearing fruit for your glory. Amen.

Musical Bonus

I love this upbeat song by Josh Wilson called *Jesus Is Alive*.

https://youtu.be/fyI-vDW_VD0

Free But Not Cheap

> In this world you will have trouble. But take
> heart! I have overcome the world.
> — JOHN 16:33

NOTE CAREFULLY WHAT JESUS *doesn't* say.

He doesn't say, "I have overcome your trouble" because that would not be true. But he does say, "I have overcome the world," which is much better anyway.

Our Lord is telling us, "Don't worry. I've got this." Our troubles come and go, and sometimes they overwhelm us. But Jesus is not overwhelmed.

He is still the Lord of all things.

Years ago, Marlene and I traveled to Jos, Nigeria, to visit some missionaries. On the final weekend of our trip, we traveled a few miles west of Jos to the Miango Rest Home.

As I walked across the grounds, I came to a lovely fieldstone church called Kirk Chapel. Behind it, I discovered the missionary graveyard. It contains about 60 graves of men and women who made the ultimate sacrifice for the sake of the gospel. Half or more of the graves are of children, most of them dying in the first few days or weeks of life.

I saw a grave with a man's name and then the dates 1919-1953. The marker read, "Placed in loving memory by his wife and children." Underneath were two words: "Abundantly Satisfied." The inscription for one young girl reads, "She is with her best friend and Lord, Jesus."

The missionary graveyard at Miango sends this message: *God's grace is free, but it is never cheap.* The missionaries and their children buried there bear testimony to the high cost of the Great Commission.

Wherever the church has gone, the cost of a new field has always been paid in blood. I saw a marker at Miango for a little child who died many years ago. The inscription read something like this: "We plant this seed in the hope that it will someday bear a harvest of souls for the Kingdom."

Jesus has overcome the world.

God help us to shine like stars so that others will see Jesus in us.

Lord Jesus, thank you for grace that is free but never cheap. And thank you for the shining example of those who have laid all on the altar of sacrifice. Grant that we might do the same for the sake of the gospel. Amen.

Musical Bonus

Hillsong Worship produced a Christmas song chock full of good theology. Let's listen to *Arrival*.

https://youtu.be/b-MwUA8Kbo4

A Time to Choose

Everyone on the side of truth listens to me.
— JOHN 18:37

THE MEN AND WOMEN of this generation have heard the name of Jesus many times. What they want to know is very simple: "Can I trust him?" In a world of religious charlatans, this is where we must begin.

Let's be clear about what we believe because we claim something the world finds incredible—literally unbelievable.

We say that when Jesus speaks, God speaks.

When Jesus speaks, his words must be obeyed.

Jesus doesn't give opinions to be discussed. His words demand a decision.

That's what makes our Lord so uncomfortable to many very nice, very upstanding religious types. They are happy to believe in a Jesus born in a manger, but if you say that he is the one and only Lord who must be worshiped and obeyed, they draw back in shock.

Worship him? Yes!

Obey him? Yes!

Follow him? Yes!

John means that Jesus Christ can be relied upon to tell the truth. When he speaks, he speaks only the truth. His words are absolutely true and authoritative. 1 Timothy 6:13 speaks of "Christ Jesus, who while testifying before Pontius Pilate, made the good confession." Jesus Christ is the supreme truth-teller, and those who want to find the truth must listen to him. I love this statement by John Watson:

"No one has yet discovered the word Jesus ought to have said, none suggested the better word he might have said. No action of his has shocked our moral sense. None has fallen short of the ideal. He is full of surprises, but they are all the surprises of perfection."

45

Everyone has to face this fundamental question about Jesus: Can I trust him? Some people will answer yes, others will say no. Until this issue is resolved, there is no point in discussing anything else.

Let's suppose you don't want to take my word for it. Read the record for yourself. Take 30 days to read Matthew, Mark, Luke, and John in the New Testament. Read the story for yourself and come to your own conclusions. Let me tell you what I believe will happen. If you read with an open mind and an open heart, you will conclude that what Jesus said is true, that he is the truth, and that his word can be eternally trusted.

I am not saying anything to try to prove it to you. I challenge you to read it for yourself. Make up your own mind. When you do, you will find that he is entirely trustworthy.

Lord Jesus, you are the truth, and you bear witness to the truth.
May I be a faithful witness for you in the eyes of the watching
world. Amen.

Musical Bonus
A group called We Are Messengers has given us a modern version of Charles Wesley's beloved *Hark! The Herald Angels Sing.*
https://youtu.be/9ZHNtZgcwoo

December 23
Paid in Full

It Is Finished.
— JOHN 19:30

DOES IT SEEM ODD to talk about the Cross two days before Christmas?

Why talk about death while we celebrate his birth?

The answer is simple: The cross was his destiny.

Fast-forward to Golgotha, Skull Hill, a place outside the walls of Jerusalem. It was located near the Damascus Road. The Romans liked to crucify people there because it guaranteed a crowd for a public execution.

Jesus has been hanging on the cross since 9 AM. At noon, darkness fell across the land. For three hours, the sun disappeared.

Whatever happened in those three hours of darkness brought Jesus to death's door. His strength is nearly gone, the struggle almost over. His chest heaves with every tortured breath; his moans now are only whispers. Instinctively, the crowd pushes closer to watch him die.

One glance at the middle cross makes clear that Jesus will not last much longer. He looks dead already. The soldiers know from years of experience that he won't make it to sundown.

They put some sour vinegar on a sponge, which they lifted to his lips on a stalk of hyssop. He moistens his lips and takes a deep breath. If you listen, you can hear the death rattle in his throat. He has less than a minute to live.

Then he speaks again. It is a quick shout—just one word. If you aren't paying attention, you miss it in all the confusion. He breathes out another sentence. Then he is dead.

What is that shout? "It is finished."

The word means "to bring to completion. The word means more than just "I survived." It means "I did exactly what I set out to do."

"It is finished" was the Savior's final cry of victory. When he died, he left no unfinished business behind. When he said, "It is finished," he was speaking the truth.

What Jesus accomplished in His death was so awesome, so total, so complete that it could never be repeated. Not even by Jesus himself. His work is "finished." There is nothing more God could do to save the human race. There is no Plan B. Plan A (the death of Christ) was good enough.

Jesus paid in full so you wouldn't have to pay anything. He finished what he came to do. If you will trust him, you will discover that in finishing his work, he paid in full the price for your sin.

Thank you, Heavenly Father, for not giving up on us when we sinned against you. Thank you for Jesus, whose death paid in full the price of our salvation. Amen.

Musical Bonus
Would you like to get into the Christmas spirit?
Check out *Gloria* by Michael W. Smith.
https://youtu.be/0p74HZUatOM

December 24
Doubters Welcome

Thomas said to him, 'My Lord and My God.'
— JOHN 20:28

THOMAS THE DOUBTER.

That's how we remember him 2000 years later. But his was not the doubt of the skeptic who refuses to believe. Thomas doubted because his heart was broken.

Jesus had died. That much was clear and undeniable. Thomas had been there in the Garden when he was arrested and taken away. He no doubt watched as the centurions hammered the nails into his hands and feet.

He must have heard Jesus scream, "My God, My God, why have you forsaken me?"

Perhaps he was there when Joseph of Arimathea took the beaten, bruised, bloody body of Jesus down from the cross. How would he ever get that image out of his mind?

He was not with the disciples because his heart had been crushed. Everything he had, he had given to Jesus, and Jesus had died.

Thomas is not an unbelieving skeptic; he is a wounded believer. He was not unwilling to believe, but unable.

One week after his resurrection, Jesus appeared to the disciples a second time. This time, Thomas was with them. Jesus speaks to him as to one whose faith is weak, not to one who has an evil heart. He said, "Put your finger here; see my hands. Reach out your hand and put it into my side. Stop doubting and believe" (John 20:27). Jesus didn't put him down. He said, "Go ahead. See for yourself. Stop doubting and believe."

As far as I can tell, Thomas never actually touched Jesus. It seems that simply seeing him face-to-face was enough to convince him. Thus do the greatest doubters often become the strongest believers. When he sees Jesus, he rises to the highest level of faith in the gospel of John as he cries out, "My Lord and my God!" (John 20:28).

David Seamands tells of a Muslim in Africa who became a Christian. When his friends asked him why he made that decision, he told them, "Suppose you were going down a road, and suddenly the road forked in two directions, and you didn't know which way to go. Then you saw two men at the fork, one dead and one alive. Which one would you follow? I decided to follow the man who is alive."

That is what we have done. We have followed the Man who is alive. Follow him and he will lead you to heaven.

Heavenly Father, on this happy Christmas Eve, grant us faith to believe all over again. Thank you for sending Jesus because he is the Savior who will lead us safely home. Amen.

Musical Bonus
Steve Green has recorded a beautiful version of *Birthday of a King / O Holy Night.* Enjoy!
https://youtu.be/rua3XpEvNn4

That You May Believe

These are written so that you may believe that
Jesus is the Christ, the Son of God, and that by
believing you may have life in His name.
— JOHN 20:31

THE DEEPEST TRUTHS ARE actually quite simple.

Years ago, the editor of the local high school newspaper interviewed me to find out what Christmas meant to me. I told her that it all comes down to one simple fact: A baby was born at Bethlehem who was God in human flesh. This is the central truth of the Christian faith—that God became a man at Christmastime. Everything else we believe derives from that essential truth.

Not everyone believes that.

That's why John's gospel comes to its climax with a reminder that the story of Jesus always leads to a decision. Our journey with John has brought us to an inescapable question: What will you do with Jesus?

Christ has come. Do you believe it?

Christ has come. Will you receive him?

In one of his sermons, Bruce Goettsche tells the delightful story of Wallace Perling—a young man who had been given a big part in the annual Christmas program. This year, he had a speaking part. He only had one line, but he was thrilled. Wallace was given the part of the Innkeeper who would turn Mary and Joseph away. His job was to answer the knock at his door, listen to the plea of Joseph, and say, "No! Begone!"

The night of the pageant finally came. Wallace had practiced hard and was ready. As the production began, he listened intently to the

Christmas story. Finally, Mary and Joseph worked their way to his door. His heart was pounding. When Wallace opened the door, there stood Mary and Joseph. They looked so tired. Joseph told how Mary was expecting a child, and they were so weary. But Wallace looked straight ahead and said, "No! Begone!"

This is where the story gets interesting. You see, Wallace didn't shut the door. Instead, he watched the couple walk dejectedly away. Finally, Wallace said, "Wait, you can have my room!"

Some thought the Christmas pageant had been ruined. But others thought it was the best Christmas program ever. This is what it means to receive Christ. You receive Jesus by opening the door and inviting him to come in.

One final word, and we are done. Perhaps you've seen the billboard with a picture of Jesus hanging on the cross. Underneath the picture are three words: "It's your move."

Jesus was born in Bethlehem. It's your move now.

Jesus died on the cross. It's your move now.

Jesus rose from the dead. It's your move now.

We end our journey by declaring our belief in Jesus, because he is God's rescue mission to humanity.

Glory to the newborn King!

Savior and Lord, on this happy Christmas Day, we rejoice at your birth. Thank you for moving into our neighborhood and becoming one with us. Glory to your name forever! Amen.

Musical Bonus
Let's wrap up our musical journey with some bluegrass gospel by a group from Alberta, Canada, called High Valley. Here's their version of *Go Tell It On the Mountain.*
https://youtu.be/ttDT0Hk9RV4

We hope you enjoyed this journey through the Advent season with us!

Would you consider donating so we could continue to offer this ebook and thousands of other resources free to people around the world through our website?

Thank you, and God bless you!

Donate to Keep Believing Ministries
https://www.keepbelieving.com/donate/